How Things Are Made

Milk to Ice Cream

By Inez Snyder

Welcome
Books™

Children's Press®
A Division of Scholastic Inc.
New York / Toronto / London / Auckland / Sydney
Mexico City / New Delhi / Hong Kong
Danbury, Connecticut

Photo Credits: Cover and all photos by Maura B. McConnell
Contributing Editor: Jennifer Silate
Book Design: Mindy Liu

Library of Congress Cataloging-in-Publication Data

Snyder, Inez.
  Milk to ice cream / by Inez Snyder.
  p. cm. — (How things are made)
  Summary: A young boy and his father make ice cream at home.
  ISBN 0-516-24268-7 (lib. bdg.) — ISBN 0-516-24360-8 (pbk.)
  1. Ice cream, ices, etc.—Juvenile literature. [1. Ice cream, ices,
  etc.] I. Title. II. Series.

  TX795 .S58 2003
  641.8'62—dc21

                                                        2002009605

Contents

Hi, my name is Mark.

My dad and I are going to make **ice cream**.

We use milk to make
ice cream.

I mix the milk and some
eggs together in a bowl.

Then, I mix sugar, flour, and salt in another bowl.

Now, Dad and I mix
everything together.

Next, Dad cooks the **mixture**.

He **stirs** the mixture while it cooks.

The mixture is finished cooking.

Dad puts in some **cream**.

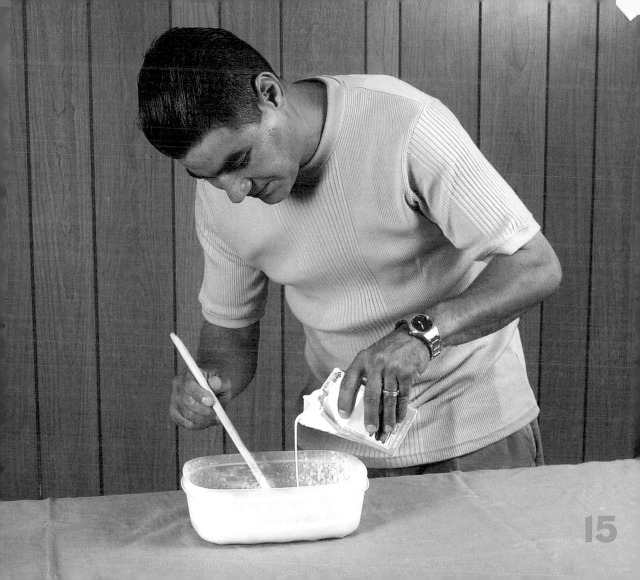

15

I add **vanilla** to the mixture.

Vanilla will make the
ice cream taste good.

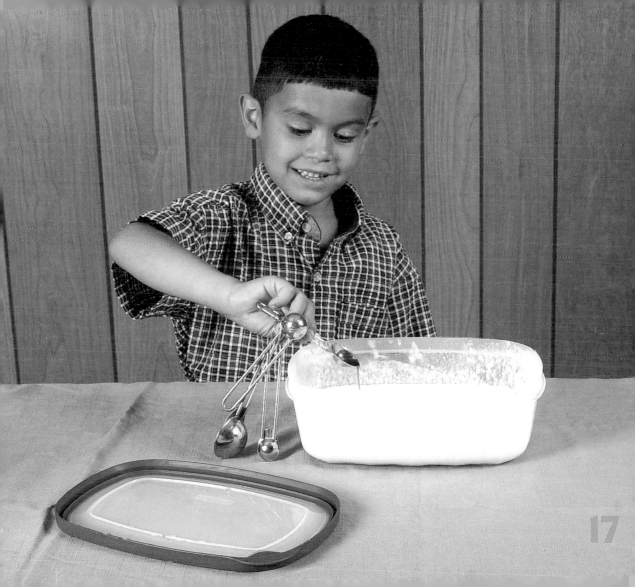

Now, Dad puts the mixture in the **freezer**.

Soon, it will be ice cream.

The ice cream is finished.

It tastes great!

New Words

cream (**kreem**) a thick, fatty liquid found in whole milk

freezer (**free**-zur) the part of a refrigerator that makes food icy or solid

ice cream (**ise kreem**) a frozen food made from milk or cream, sugar or honey, and sometimes eggs

mixture (**miks**-chur) something made from different things mixed together

stirs (**stuhrz**) when someone mixes something by moving it around in a container with a spoon or a stick

vanilla (vuh-**nil**-uh) a flavor that comes from the seed of a plant, and is used in ice cream, cakes, and other foods

To Find Out More

Books
From Cow to Ice Cream
by Bertram T. Knight
Children's Press

Ice Cream
by Jules Older
Charlesbridge Publishing

Web Site
Ice Cream: an Education
http://www.ice-cream.org/school/index.htm
Learn about the history of ice cream and play games on this Web site.

Index

cream, 14

freezer, 18

ice cream, 4, 6, 16, 18, 20

mixture, 12, 14, 16, 18

stirs, 12

vanilla, 16

About the Author

Inez Snyder writes and edits children's books. She also enjoys painting and cooking for her family.

Reading Consultants

Kris Flynn, Coordinator, Small School District Literacy, The San Diego County Office of Education

Shelly Forys, Certified Reading Recovery Specialist, W.J. Zahnow Elementary School, Waterloo, IL

Sue McAdams, Former President of the North Texas Reading Council of the IRA, and Early Literacy Consultant, Dallas, TX